W9-BLN-365

Lac Courte Oreilles
Elementary Library

Property of L.C.O. SCHOOL

A DORLING KINDERSLEY BOOK
Conceived, edited, and designed by DK Direct Limited

Note to parents

What's Inside? Plants is designed to help
young children understand how plants grow and flower.
It illustrates what is inside a rosebud, how a pitcher
plant catches its food, and how a cactus survives on very
little water. It is a book for you and your child to read
and talk about together, and to enjoy.

Designers Juliette Norsworthy and Sonia Whillock
Typographic Designer Nigel Coath
US Editor B. Alison Weir
Editor Sarah Phillips
Design Director Ed Day
Editorial Director Jonathan Reed

Illustrator Richard Manning
Photographer Matthew Ward
Photograph page 15 Stephen Dalton/NHPA
Writer Angela Royston

First American Edition, 1992
10 9 8 7 6 5 4 3 2 1

Dorling Kindersley, Inc., 232 Madison Avenue
New York, New York 10016

Copyright © 1992 Dorling Kindersley Limited, London.

All rights reserved under International and Pan-American Copyright Conventions.
Published in the United States by Dorling Kindersley, Inc., New York, New York. Distributed by Houghton
Mifflin Company, Boston, Massachusetts. Published in Great Britain by Dorling Kindersley Limited, London.
No part of this publication may be reproduced, stored in a retrieval system, or transmitted in any form
or by any means, electronic, mechanical, photocopying, recording or otherwise,
without the prior written permission of the copyright owner.

Library of Congress Cataloging-in-Publication Data
Plants. – 1st American ed.
    p. cm. – (What's inside?)
Summary: Examines the inner workings of various plants,
including the tulip, cactus, and thistle.
ISBN 1-56458-005-9
1. Plants – Juvenile literature. 2. Botany – Anatomy – Juvenile literature.
[1. Plants. 2. Botany.] I. Dorling Kindersley, Inc. II. Series.
QK49.P53 1992
581 — dc20   91–58214
                                                      CIP
                                                      AC
Printed in Italy

WHAT'S INSIDE?

PLANTS

Property of L.C.O. SCHOOL

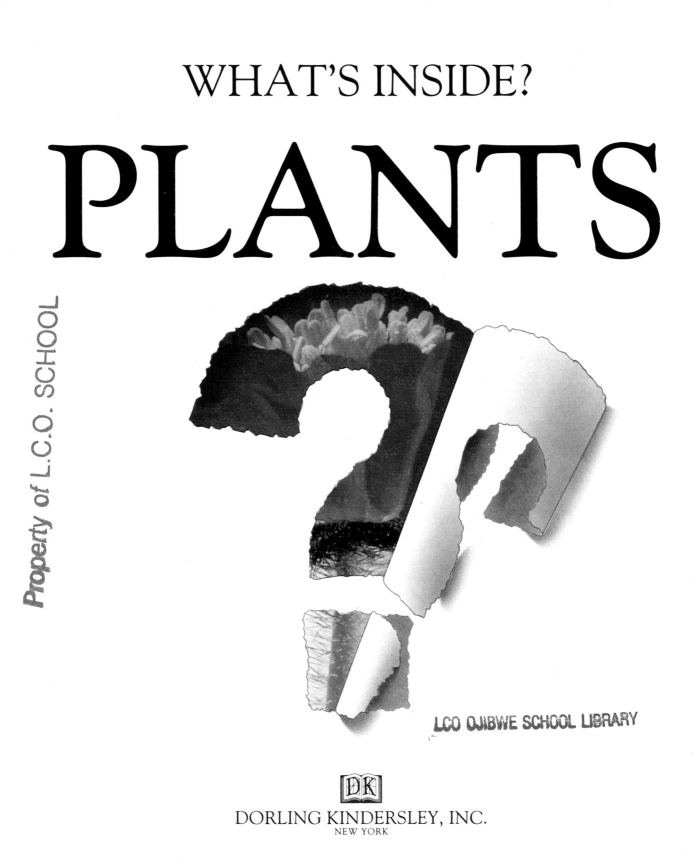

LCO OJIBWE SCHOOL LIBRARY

DK

DORLING KINDERSLEY, INC.
NEW YORK

ROSEBUD

Soon, this bud will blossom into a sweet-smelling rose. Like all plants and flowers, roses need water and sunlight to live and grow.

Oil in the petals gives the rose its sweet smell, which attracts bees.

These special leaves, called sepals, kept the bud safe while it grew.

This strong stalk holds the leaves and flowers up to the light.

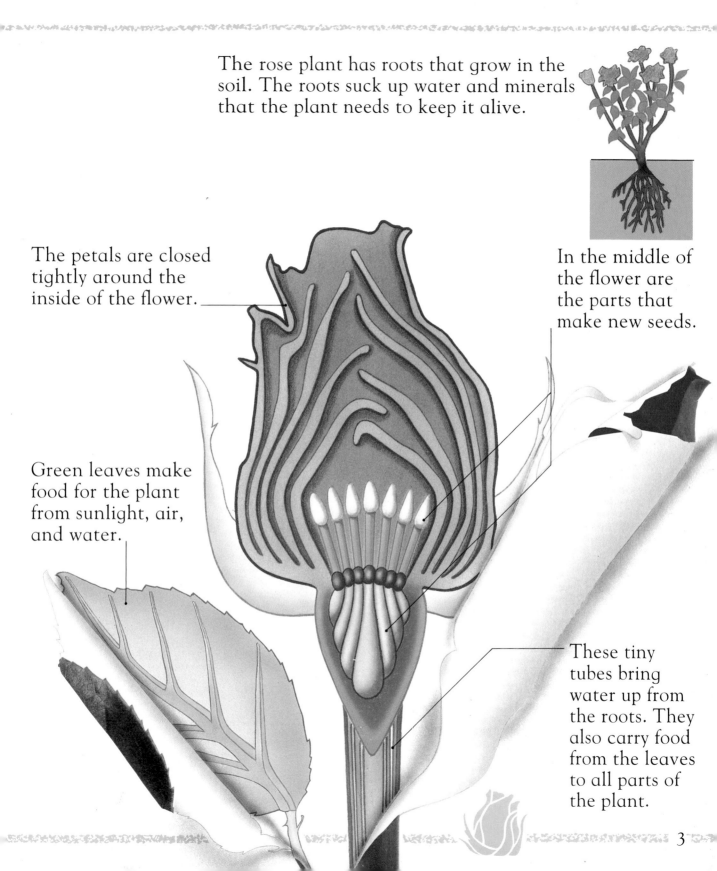

The rose plant has roots that grow in the soil. The roots suck up water and minerals that the plant needs to keep it alive.

The petals are closed tightly around the inside of the flower.

In the middle of the flower are the parts that make new seeds.

Green leaves make food for the plant from sunlight, air, and water.

These tiny tubes bring water up from the roots. They also carry food from the leaves to all parts of the plant.

3

TULIP

Tulips flower in the spring. Bees go from flower to flower collecting nectar and pollen. Bees collect pollen to make honey, but flowers also need it to make new seeds.

The five brightly colored petals attract bees. They open in warm, sunny weather when bees are buzzing around.

The petals are thick and waxy. They close up at night and when it rains, to keep the inside safe and dry.

The tulip's leaves are long and thin.

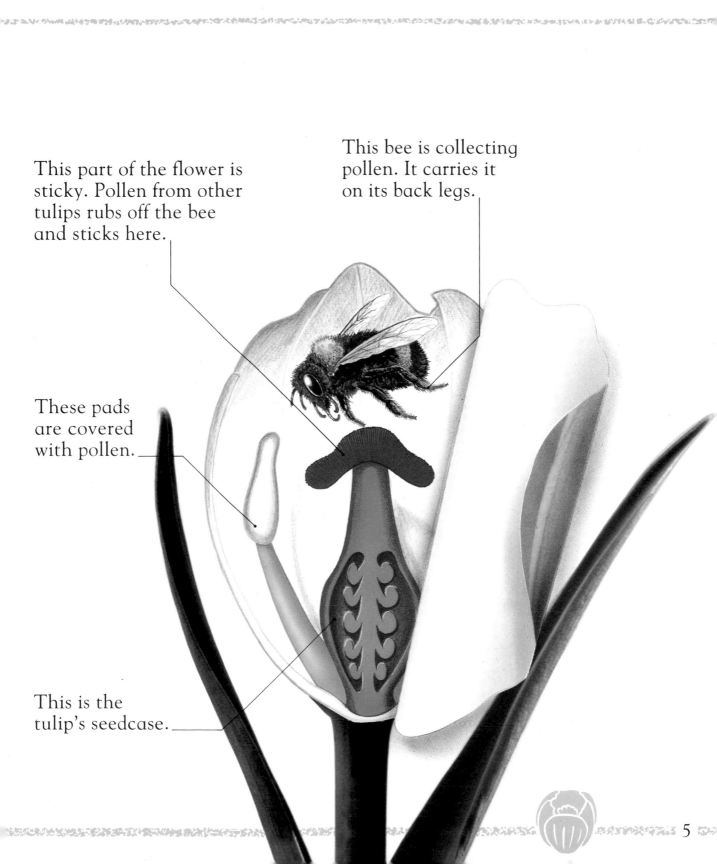

This part of the flower is sticky. Pollen from other tulips rubs off the bee and sticks here.

This bee is collecting pollen. It carries it on its back legs.

These pads are covered with pollen.

This is the tulip's seedcase.

POPPY

This beautiful poppy grows wild in fields of wheat. Its flowers do not last long. The petals soon fall off, leaving behind a bundle of seeds.

These yellow pads are covered with pollen. When a bee comes to the flower, some of the pollen sticks to the hairs on the bee's legs.

The petals are like tissue paper. When the poppy's seeds are ready to grow, the petals dry up and fall off.

The stalk is covered with fine hairs. These prevent caterpillars and other insects from crawling up the stalk to eat the poppy.

The seedcase has rows of little holes around the top, just like a salt shaker. When the wind blows hard enough, the seeds fall out and scatter. New poppies may grow where the seeds fall.

Bees bring pollen from other poppies which sticks to the top of the seedcase.

The seedcase is full of seeds waiting for grains of pollen to start them growing.

Each grain of pollen grows a tube down into the seedcase. When the tube reaches a seed, the grain of pollen moves down the tube and joins with the seed.

LCO OJIBWE SCHOOL LIBRARY

7

CACTUS

This cactus is growing in a pot, but it usually grows in hot, dry places, like deserts. A cactus can live for months without rain by storing water inside its stem.

This is the cactus's stem.

The spines of the cactus are really its leaves. If it had ordinary leaves, they would dry up in the hot sun.

The tough skin stops the water inside from leaking out.

Cactus flowers often bloom when it rains. The seeds are made inside the flower.

These big spines stop animals and birds from eating the plant to steal the water stored inside.

When the soil gets wet, the roots suck water into the stem.

Do not water a cactus too often! The inside of the stem is already full of water.

THISTLE

Thistles grow on grassy ground. They are covered with spikes and prickles, and are very difficult to pick! In the flowerhead, lots of small flowers are packed tightly together.

The thistle is actually made up of many tiny flowers, or florets.

More flowers are forming under this hard, spiky covering.

The spines protect the thistle from animals that want to eat it.

The leaves are very sharp so that animals leave them alone.

When the seeds are ready, they float away on tiny parachutes of fine, white hairs. Some of them will grow into new plants.

There may be as many as 100 florets in the flowerhead.

There is a seed at the bottom of each tiny flower.

The hard stalk is full of milky sap. Sap contains the thistle's food.

PITCHER PLANT

Many plants are eaten by animals, but with the pitcher plant it is the other way around. It eats insects! Pitcher plants grow high up in trees, and live by catching and eating insects in special traps.

This trapdoor opens on bright days when there are lots of insects around. When it rains, it closes to keep out the water.

Sweet nectar is made around the rim. This attracts insects to the trap.

The pitcher plant's trap grows from the end of its leaf.

Insects are attracted to the pitcher plant's bright color.

The pitcher plant has lots of traps to make sure it gets enough food.

The rim of the trap is slippery, so that the insects fall in.

The wall of the trap is waxy and smooth, so that the insects can't climb out.

Insects drown in this liquid at the bottom of the trap.

The insects are slowly digested in the liquid, just as food is digested in your stomach.

BROMELIAD

Bromeliads live in the hot, wet rain forests of South America. They grow high up on the branches of trees and when it rains, each collects its own little tank of water.

The leaves are long, thin, and tough. They have a jagged edge to prevent animals from eating them.

New leaves are red at first. They grow out from the center of the plant.

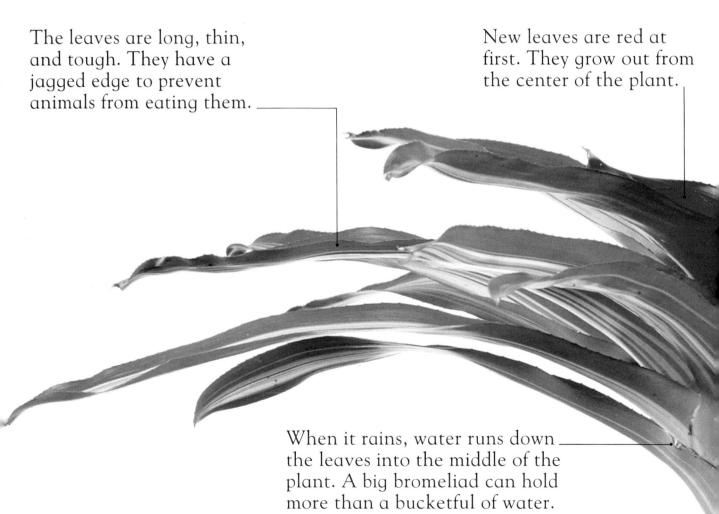

When it rains, water runs down the leaves into the middle of the plant. A big bromeliad can hold more than a bucketful of water.

A bromeliad doesn't take in water from the ground. It takes it from its own water tank.

This small frog lives in the tank of water. Sometimes tadpoles and insects live here, too.

Bromeliads attach themselves to other plants with their short roots.

15

WATER LILY

Water lilies grow in lakes and ponds where the water is shallow.
They float on the surface and have all the water they need.

Water lilies have
big, flat leaves
that float like
little rafts.

This is the flower.
The petals grow in a
spiral, with the smallest
one at the center.

The leaves are
tough and waxy
so water just
runs off them.

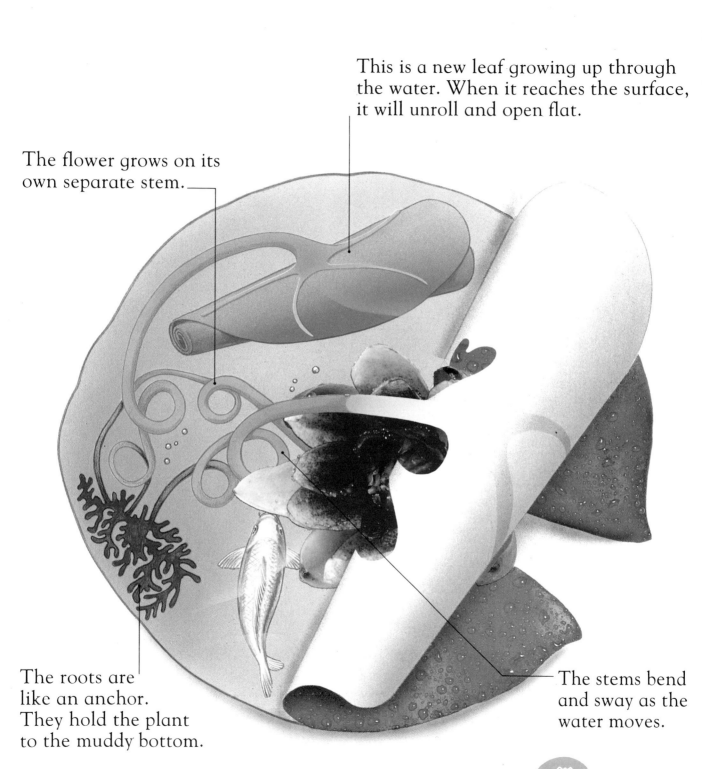

This is a new leaf growing up through the water. When it reaches the surface, it will unroll and open flat.

The flower grows on its own separate stem.

The roots are like an anchor. They hold the plant to the muddy bottom.

The stems bend and sway as the water moves.